UNDER WINTER SKIES

Also by Henry Marsh

A First Sighting, ISBN 9780951447017
first published in Great Britain in 2005 by Maclean Dubois.

A Turbulent Wake, ISBN 9780951447048
first published in Great Britain in 2007 by Maclean Dubois.

A Trail of Dreaming, ISBN 97809556114105
Poems to accompany an exhibition of Australian landscape paintings
by Kym Needle, published 2009 by the Open Eye Gallery.

The Guidman's Daughter, ISBN 9780951447062
first published in Great Britain in 2009 by Maclean Dubois
distributed by Birlinn.

The Hammer and the Fire, ISBN 9780956527829
first published in Great Britain in 2011 by Maclean Dubois
distributed by Birlinn.

Painted Trees, ISBN 9780956114112
Poems to accompany an exhibition of Australian landscape paintings
by Kym Needle, published 2012 by the Open Eye Gallery.

A Voyage to Babylon, ISBN 9780956527844
first published in Great Britain in 2013 by Maclean Dubois
distributed by Birlinn.

The Bedrock, ISBN 9780956527851
first published in Great Britain in 2015 by Maclean Dubois.

UNDER WINTER SKIES

THE LAST JOURNEY OF THE GREAT MARQUIS

HENRY MARSH

In memory of Jackie, my beloved wife
1948–2016

Maclean Dubois

This edition first published in hardback in Great Britain in 2017
by Maclean Dubois
14/2 Gloucester Place, Edinburgh EH3 6EF

ISBN: 978 0 95652 786 8

British Library Cataloguing-in-Publication Data
A catalogue record for this book is available on request
from the British Library.

Designed and typeset in Garamond by Abigail Salvesen
Printed and bound by TJ International

ACKNOWLEDGEMENTS

I am most grateful to the following for their very helpful comments and advice: Dr Catriona MacDonald, Reader in Early Modern History at the University of Glasgow; Professor Christopher Whatley, Professor of History, University of Dundee; Lt. Col. Malcolm MacVitie, Chairman of the 1st Marquis of Montrose Society; George Harris, historian and old colleague; my daughters, who tried to ensure that my efforts were more or less intelligible, and to Ronald Black, who, in the blessing given by the clansman in 'A Pack of Naked Runagates', very kindly translated the first couplet into Gaelic.

I am also very grateful for the Isabel Dalhousie Fellowship, set up by Alexander McCall Smith, which gave me time and space to research the history of the 1st Marquis at the Institute for Advanced Studies in the Humanities at the University of Edinburgh.

CONTENTS

INTRODUCTION

In touching upon the story of the 1st Marquis of Montrose and the Wars of the Three Kingdoms it has been in my mind that Scotland, for a time, was a theocracy driven by fanatics for whom the rule of law counted for nothing against their vision of the laws of God, derived mostly from the darker precepts of the Old Testament. It was a country gripped by brutal, concurrent civil wars, both tribal and sectarian, all sides characterised by atrocities – and this but a few generations ago. What was it like for folk to be swept up in such events utterly beyond their control?

It little behoves us to look on with righteous disbelief as sectarian strife, civil wars and atrocities unfold in our own times. We are largely separated by geography from the worst of it, though from time to time, the savagery strikes at our own communities. Peering through the back door of history, however hard things are to discern, at least we can recognise the motivations that drive us to extremism and civil war and humbly acknowledge that there we have been.

FAMILY

James Graham – the Graham – was born in 1612 into an old and distinguished family. When he was fourteen his father died and James became the 5th Earl of Montrose. His sister, Margaret, had married Archibald, Lord Napier, a son of John Napier, the eminent scientist and mathematician who discovered logarithms. After the death of James' father, Archibald became the young earl's tutor and cast a fatherly eye on him. The Napiers were to provide important personal support for James in future years and his nephew, Archibald, the second Lord Napier, would become a staunch friend.

Intelligent, well-read, well-educated, as a young man James inherited huge estates. The great swathe of their lands stretched from

Montrose in the north down through the Ochils and Strathearn, to Kincardine Castle and Mugdock Castle in Strathblane. He spent liberally and dressed in the latest fashion – he liked to cut a dash. Amongst his favourite reading was Lucan's *Pharsalia*, the wars of Caesar, Quintus Curtius' *Life of Alexander the Great* and he was fascinated by Sir Walter Raleigh's *History of the World*. It was clear that even as a young man he was predisposed to seek out honour and glory. He also wrote accomplished poetry.

To complete his education, for three years, from 1633 to 1636, he travelled in France, Germany and Italy studying the arts of war and particularly the campaigns, tactics and strategies of Gustavus Adolphus, the great Swedish general.

He had been married young, in 1629, to Magdalen, the youngest daughter of David, Lord Carnegie, Earl of Southesk. They had four children. The eldest, John, died aged fourteen during his father's winter campaign of 1645. James, who would become the 2nd Marquis, was imprisoned as a boy for some time in Edinburgh Castle. During her husband's campaigns and period of exile, the two younger children, Robert and Jean, lived with their mother on her father's estate at Kinnaird Castle near Montrose. In effect, Lord Carnegie became their guardian. Magdalen would have seen her husband only rarely. No personal correspondence between them has survived.

James Graham proved to be a brilliant soldier who earned a European-wide reputation but he did not have, perhaps, the temperament to be a statesman – he seemed to be impatient of nuance, of ambiguity, of different opinions. He lived by his ideals and expected others to live by them also – there was, then, a touch of inherent blindness, of arrogance.

THE SCOTTISH NATIONAL COVENANT

In 1637, when Charles I attempted to impose bishops and *The Booke of Common Prayer* – the 'English' Prayer Book – on the people of Scotland he provoked outrage. Montrose, in protest – he was a passionate Presbyterian – became one of the first signatories of the Scottish National Covenant. It demanded that the Scottish Parliament and the General Assembly should be freed from Charles' interference and that bishops should be removed from office so that, in effect, the power of the Kirk and the nobility would be enhanced, thereby diminishing the power of the king. The period of extreme repression that followed led, ultimately, to the Wars of the Three Kingdoms – a period that was once designated 'The English Civil War'.

The issues for young Montrose were of liberty and freedom of worship for all, but he failed to anticipate how such freedoms would feed the ambitions of the Kirk's fanatics. His brother-in-law, Lord Napier, did not sign. Montrose fought against Charles I in the First Bishops' War as a general in the Scottish Covenanting army.

In June 1639, the king made peace with the Covenanters in the Pacification of Berwick. He agreed to call an Assembly of the Kirk and a free Scottish Parliament. But the hard-line Covenanters began to assert themselves and some ministers orchestrated social unrest and violence for their own political purposes. Meanwhile, the covenanting Archibald, Earl of Argyll, chief of Clan Campbell, sought to gain ascendency in the Scottish Parliament. Nevertheless, it was Montrose who, in 1640, led the first foray of the Covenanting army into England in the Second Bishops' War. The Treaty of Berwick had been short-lived.

After the war Montrose was arrested on the grounds that he had conspired against the Argyll-led Committee of the Estates. In 1640 he had signed the Cumbernauld Bond swearing allegiance both to the Covenant and to the king and opposing the 'practicking of a few'

– namely Argyll and his faction. He was imprisoned in Edinburgh Castle then released on bail and retired to his estates for a few years.

CHANGE OF ALLEGIANCE

In 1643, during the First English Civil War, the Scots accepted The Solemn League and Covenant whereby they agreed to support the beleaguered English Parliamentarians in their opposition to King Charles. The price of their military assistance was the promise that the English Parliament would seek to establish a Presbyterian system in England. In other words, the true price was the establishment of a Presbyterian hegemony. Whereas, the National Covenant had sought freedom to worship according to Presbyterian precepts and was, thereby, enthusiastically supported by Montrose, The Solemn League and Covenant sought to impose the Kirk's Presbyterianism on England. It was the difference between freedom and compulsion and a symptom of the Kirk's slide into extremism. The promise of The Solemn League was, in any event, entirely unrealistic. Nevertheless, in 1644 the Scots sent an army into England in support of Cromwell and the Parliamentarians.

Montrose became fiercely opposed to the Solemn League and worked for an alliance of the Scottish and English parliaments against Cromwell – now the common enemy. Consequently, he had joined Charles at Oxford in 1643. This was a momentous decision for Montrose. Amongst his principle motives was his fear of Argyll's overweening ambition – he had become, in effect, the dictator of Scotland. Indeed, Argyll would become known as 'King Campbell'. A consequence for Montrose, however, was that he would now be regarded as a traitor to the National Covenant and to the Kirk.

In order to distract the Covenanters from supporting Cromwell in England, Montrose began a campaign in Scotland with the support of Alasdair MacColla – otherwise, Alexander MacDonald – who led an alliance of Irish MacDonalds and Scottish Highlanders, notably the MacDonalds and their allies. However, in the atmosphere inspired by covenanting zeal, that Montrose should seek the assistance of Irish 'papists' was incendiary.

MacColla proved to be a superb battle commander who, reputedly, initiated the devastating Highland Charge. Their common enemy was the Marquis of Argyll and his Campbells. There began what was, in effect, a vicious Gaelic civil war that Montrose would use for his own Royalist purposes.

There followed a series of brilliant Montrose and MacColla victories, largely dependent on war-hardy Irish and Highland troops. They were splendidly mobile and entirely at home in the hills and mountains to which they could retreat when in difficulties. They excelled in what was, in effect, guerrilla warfare.

The weakness of this alliance was that they fought in their time-honoured manner and following their victories they would desert, returning home with their spoils. The Graham's army would melt away – and they had no taste for campaigns in the domain of their hereditary and sectarian enemies in the Lowlands. Together with woeful intelligence and fickle Lowland nobles, this lead to the Graham's disastrous defeat at Philiphaugh. He would never win another battle.

EXILE

In July 1646, Charles surrendered himself to the Covenanters and Montrose was ordered to cease his activities. In September 1646, he sailed into exile and joined the court of Queen Henrietta Maria, wife of Charles I, in Paris. His reputation had preceded him thanks to an account of his campaigns written by his Chaplain, George Wishart. Cardinal de Retz wrote that Montrose was, 'the only man in the world who has ever brought to my mind such heroes as we read of in the pages of Plutarch.' Such was his fame as a soldier that, if he had chosen, he could have become a Marshall of France.

However, dismayed by the corruption and in-fighting of the exiled court, he moved for a time to the court of Elizabeth of Bohemia in The Hague. Elizabeth was the eldest sister of Charles I, highly intelligent and cultivated. Under the patronage of her husband, Archduke Ferdinand, Montrose became a Marshall of the Holy Roman Empire – which allowed him to raise troops for Charles' purposes in continental Europe. Elizabeth's court also brought him into contact with one of her daughters, Princess Louise. Magdalen, the wife of Montrose, had died in November 1645, and there is a tantalising scrap of evidence to suggest that a relationship might have developed between Louise and Montrose.

He was in Germany trying to raise troops for a return to Scotland when he heard that Argyll and his faction had sold King Charles to Cromwell on the promise that Presbyterianism would, indeed, be established in England and for a substantial amount of the money that was owing to the Scots army. Argyll and the Duke of Hamilton each pocketed £30,000. Then in January 30th, 1649, Charles was executed in London. The effect on Montrose was profound. It produced a passionate, steely resolution in him. Nothing would deflect him – let alone the prospect of dying for his cause.

When he met the new king, Charles II, at The Hague, Montrose offered a plan to invade Scotland with an army drawn from European sources. However, the Argyll faction had sent a deputation to negotiate terms for Charles' return. Faced with two options, the King decided to take up the Montrose offer and Charles then made him Lieutenant Governor of Scotland. Montrose went to North Germany and Scandinavia to raise his army.

RETURN TO SCOTLAND

In March 1650, he sailed for Orkney but lost troops and two ammunition ships in a storm. He arrived on the mainland early in April with his army augmented by Orkney conscripts. Unfortunately, the young, inexperienced and fickle Charles, had continued to explore negotiations with the Argyll faction. Perhaps his intention was to use the Montrose landing to exert pressure on the Covenanters in their negotiations, but at the same time he gave formal recognition to Argyll who then moved to put a price on the Graham's head in the name of the king.

Perhaps the best that can be said of the eighteen-year-old Charles was that he was out of his depth in these negotiations. More probably, weighing up his best chances, it was a straight-forward betrayal. And Montrose knew it. Who in Scotland would support him in these circumstances? It was his death warrant.

Montrose and his troops were routed at Carbisdale. In a time of desperate need there was no Alasdair MacColla to call upon. Montrose had his horse shot from under him. Wounded he made his way into the hills. It was unknown territory. Lost, he found himself at Ardvreck castle on the north shore of Loch Assynt. There, according to your point of view, he was 'betrayed' by MacLeod of Assynt.

Brought to Parliament in Edinburgh, there was no trial, merely a long discourse from the Lord Chancellor that confronted him with his various crimes and rebellions. Then his sentence was pronounced. He was condemned to be hanged and quartered in a public execution at the Mercat Cross – he would have expected to be 'headed'. He died on the afternoon of 21st May, 1650. He was thirty seven years old.

HIS LAST JOURNEY

In these poems I follow Montrose from Ardvreck Castle in Assynt, where he was captured, to Skibo Castle, west of Dornoch in Sutherland. From there he and his escort make their way through Moray and by the Bog of Gight where his eldest son, John, Lord Graham, had been buried at Bellie Kirk in 1645. They proceed through Keith and eventually pass near Stonehaven into the Mearns. It was from Stonehaven that the Graham had set sail into exile in 1646. At Kinnaird Castle, a few miles west of Montrose – home territory for the Graham – he is permitted to say farewells to his remaining children. In Monifieth he makes a daring attempt at escape but, failing, he is taken the few miles to Dundee, the town he had sacked five years before. I have found only one source that suggests that he was then put on a ship for Leith – but I have taken that up.

Into this sequence I have interpolated retrospective scenes and events but each poem is dated to help the reader establish a chronology.

UNDER WINTER SKIES

AT OLD MONTROSE

A grey weight of stillness
lies across the Basin.
Rushes are ghosted in rime.
A seal's head rises
like a random thought.
A dozen Whoopers delve,
take to the air. After their rush
and wheep, dusk settles.

Down in the town,
by his birthplace,
the Marquis is cast in bronze.
In the crystal night meteors
fall out of the Lion.
They burn, for their moment,
over his head. Pass
into dust. Frost grows.

ASSYNT

After the Battle of Carbisdale
27th April, 1650

Wounded, fevered, Montrose
tramps unknown hills.
A Highland April – Spring showers
falling as driving sleet.
He watches the certainties of light
dissolving into darkness.

He'd seen men drowning
in the Kyle, slaughtered in flight.
Should he stand and fall?
Given a horse he was able to ride
then chose to walk, pass
like a shadow through copse and howe.

After Philiphaugh, reprisals
were savage and friends
and fellow officers were hanged
but at least he could see
his way – went north
in hope to raise another army.

But Carbisdale was abject.
Wind and wave had conspired
with a devious king – munition
ships sank off Orkney. Perhaps
a whispering secret in his soul

demanded heroic failure.
Careless intelligence, fickle
clans – they had read the wind's
direction. His horse was shot
from under him. Wounded, he fought
free, threw Star and Garter
under the thorns of a whin.

Round and round the scenes recur.
Out-thought by Colonel Strachan
who'd led as once the Graham
had done. The Orkney troops
had run away. What price
a MacColla Highland charge?

His few companions have gone
their different ways. He staggers
west by north – towards Assynt?
Nights he spends shaking,
huddled in a sodden plaid.
'I suffer as I have inflicted.'

To escape Covenant troopers,
he'd sought a shepherd's help –
hid under a sheep trough.
Vows never again to put an innocent
man at risk. Perhaps, in the end,
it's our kindnesses that save us.
Moor on moor stretches

winter-brown and a maze
of pools and peat hags.
A deer skull marks
where an exhausted beast had foundered.
He gnaws his gloves in hunger.

The bone-bleached roots
of ancient trees are monumental.
The wind is singing as it scourges.
Now mind and landscape meet
in an overwhelming moment –
is this the true defeat?

What threshold does he cross?
It seems the Bodach guides him
climbing, climbing, step
by stone step into – release.
And the Grey Man shining, resolving
out of darkness into splintering light.

Now looming through sleet
Ardvreck Castle and a ghost
from the hills, filthy in blood
and glaur. A gillie has found him.
He can hardly speak.
MacLeod of Assynt will help him.

MONTROSE AND BLACK PATE AT BLAIR ATHOLL

29th–30th August 1644

Dreamlike, from the shimmering hills,
two Highland gentlemen – trews,
short coats, plaids at the shoulder,
broadswords and targes. Montrose,
in his bonnet, wears a sprig of oats.
They'd walked thirty miles from Perth
avoided tracks by Tay and Tummel.

Athollmen, raised by the fiery cross
have gathered at Blair Atholl to confront
a host of Irish caterans. More
than the Tilt flows between them.
The men of Atholl howl and strain
like leashed hounds. Unmoved
by the turmoil, Montrose addresses the Irish.
This slight young man shows
the King's commission to the giant MacColla.

The Ulster MacDonalds cheer, fire
a ragged volley. The Athollmen
brandish their weapons, hurl
execrations against the papist reivers.

The moment is poised on a breath.

His companion jumps into the Tilt
and wades towards them –
Black Pate, Patrick Graham
the younger, the Marquis's first recruit.
He's recognised by Robertsons and Stewarts.
Will they make this unlikely alliance?

Then calm, utterly assured, the King's
Lieutenant speaks. The spell is cast –
heads and hearts are won.
All join in a great shout:
'No more of King Campbell.
All for King Stuart.' And a salvo –
of bonnets – in the air. Through the tumult
an exultant pibroch searches along the hills.

Next morning, near the house of Lude
Montrose raises the royal standard.

He has an army – far fewer than he'd hoped –
some half-starved, some armed
with sticks – but civil war is engendered.

What did it cost him – a Covenant general
taking arms against the Covenant?
In the hot, dark room of that night
he saw Scotland's sons strewn,
the slaughter. But soon after sunrise,
as he'd stood in the quiet and cool

of the garden at Lude looking down
on the Strath of Atholl ringed
by mountains, their glens and gullies
flowing with light, he'd felt
his heart stound, for it seemed
that the land itself was with him.

DONALD IAIN MACDONALD OF KNOIDART

Kilsyth
15th August, 1645

Beasts lolling in the meadows.
Heather slopes loud with bees.
The sun hot on our backs –
that blue, endless. But our stomachs
churn for this strange visitation
about to fall through the everyday.
For here the world ends
for some of us. His winnowing fork
is in His hand. But tomorrow
the sun will rise, the bees
will be working – the river running.

It begins. Shoulders hunched,
targes over our heads, we charge
in our sarks up the slope to the ridge
above Banton burn, loup
dykes and enclosures. Nervous,
they fire too soon – and over
our heads. We fall on with broadsword,
targe, and gralloching dirk.
Our Lochaber axe-men lope and
hew. They've tried to outflank us –
we break through their column.
But their right flank holds
on the hill. Covenant regulars

reinforce their line. We fight
to a standstill – that weight
against us. Their cuirassiers attack,
war-hardy lancers. Then something
more than horseman, uncanny –
rider on a pale horse –
the charmed Earl of Airlie spurs
up the slope. Fired by his purpose,
the Royalist cavalry follow.

From the strewn howe the Covenant
falls back – that singing moment.
The Graham orders a general attack.
Their trumpets sound retreat.

They run. Swift as fire along
August hills – roaring, exultant
on the wind – we follow. Gutted,
headed, hearts failing, they fall.

We butcher, pitiless, tireless,
our sarks stiff with their blood.

Montrose is Master of Scotland.

ROBERT FERRIER, FIFE LEVIES

Kilsyth

No. It's not like that –
there's no glory in it.

At the heart of the chaos
you're blind
                to what's happening.
Just men you must kill –
or be killed.
             You're soaked
in sweat, your sword arm
leaden,
      you struggle
to keep your feet,
staggering
          among dead
and wounded,
             the stinking
offal. You hack
and stab
       and still
they come,
         relentless.

I'm lucky, lost teeth to the edge of a targe
and half an ear. I was up on the howe,
our regular regiments crushing behind us,
driving us to our slaughter. Wild

12

as a bear, a cateran got amongst us wielding
two swords. Broken pike staffs
were stuck in the targe on his back. Madness
in his eyes, foam at the mouth – Goliath
of Gath set free from the pit. No one
could touch him. Their cavalry charged.

Necks
        stretched,
nostrils
        flared,
eyes
     rolling,
their horses
                plough
through us.
                A wounded
horse
        screams,
rears,
        hooves
scrabbling
                at the air.
Our line
            collapses.
We scatter.
                The Irish
come howling after.

'Unfit for service,' the officer had said.

'No skill in arms.' But I'd wit enough
to escape the shambles, crawled up a burn,
heart thumping, breath rasping,
coat and boots thrown off – half
naked. A nail-maker from Kirkcaldy –
what in the Deil's name was I doing there?

I hid in a burn under the turf of a bank –
a place where a shadowy trout might lie.
After an hour I was shaking with cold,
crawled out into the sun and saw below
a cluster of cottar's houses. The Irishes
had set them burning. As folk staggered out
they were felled. To what purpose?
Women were screaming like stricken animals.
They left, driving the guidman's cattle.

 Hunger
  finds
courage. I wait
for the forenicht,
   climb
down into a haunted
silence.
  Blue
ghosts
 hover,
catch at the throat.
The waft
  of a breeze

sets flames
flickering
           along a rafter.

I've seen miners
crushed, a skull
smashed in the foundry –
but here is a cottar
slung over a trestle,
his throat wide-gaping
like a slaughtered pig.

Somewhere a child
begins begins to cry.

They say Montrose
is the Antichrist.

AT SKIBO CASTLE

5th May, 1650

Assynt's wife had received him –
MacLeod of Assynt betrayed him.

Bound hand and foot
to an old garron he's taken
lumbering back through the hills
towards Dornoch. Wounds throb.
That wincing jar. Fevered,
he hovers in his mind's twilight.

The escort arrives at Skibo Castle.
They're met by the Dowager Lady Grey.
At table, General Holbourn
sits at the Lady's right hand.

'She taks her leg o'mutton
and skelps him roun the lug wi it.
He coups frae his chair, an' she
in her best imperial manner –
"Ye'll nae sit at my richt haun
my mannie when a Marquis is at my table."
And the general on his doup in the gravy
wi his wig roon his een. The Graham,
grave as a ghost, taks his seat
wi'a bow to my ladyship. Though
I caucht the glint o' a smile.

Losh me – laugh. The kitchen
was in sik a roar. Hamish
says that e'n in the Laird's day
she aye wore the breeks.'

THROUGH MORAY

May, 1650

May – but he travels
under winter skies
leaden with failure.
Untreated wounds –
the grey eyes
glitter with fever.

But as the sun will steal
through February murk –
that first, elusive,
hint of warmth –
a few old friends
attend him, and at Elgin,
the parson of Duffus
a dear, fond face,
a fellow student
from St Andrews.

Farewells –
then they're locked
forever in the past.

Though near
the Bog of Gight,
the past unlocks –
John, Lord Graham,
his eldest son,

was interred
at Bellie kirk.
Fourteen years old.

That winter campaign –
the winter that killed
his exhausted child.

Or was it the blind father?

INVERLOCHY

'He whose house is burned becomes a soldier.'

Gaelic proverb

2nd February, 1645

Through the wind's turmoil, battering snow.
A deer lies dead in a corrie. Ribs
gape to the eagle's beak. No fleetness
of limb could carry it beyond this cold.
Flesh freezes. A man would hope for burial.

We lie together and let snow cover us.
Our death's rehearsal? Who would dare sleep?

At dawn the wind shifts sou'west. By noon
the burns are trickling. But the snow feet thick.
We plunge to our chests through crusted drifts.

Keppoch shepherds guide us. We begin
to wonder. Gaunt with cold and hunger
we spend this night on the Braes of Ben Nevis.

As the Pibroch of Donuil Dhu rouses to battle,
the sons of Ranald distil out of darkness,
flow down the slopes. Campbell clansmen catch
the Graham's banner flaunting across the dawn.
What black art brought the Devil through the snow?
Surf-roar of battle cries, thunder of foot
and hoof – that overwhelming tide.

Men matched in suffering and in valour –
at what moment does the spirit break,
the will know its triumph? They harvest
the Bog Myrtle, swathes are cut low.
Headless, a corpse twitches, its impatient
fingers scrabble at the earth. A Maclean
sword thrusts through a throat – flood
at the mouth. They slaughter along the shore
of Loch Eil. Through clenched teeth
last breaths hiss. Failing eyes
see the troubled wake of Campbell's galley –
their chief absconding on black wings.

Fifteen hundred souls – and the air
thick with their passage. Gull flocks gather.
Stab. The stretched sea eagle
folds and tears. And Johnny Graham
stood witness, his face ice-scorched,
lips blue. Boy in a man's battle.

SERMON

Master William Kinanmond
Keith, 12th May, 1650

His zeal has been not only for the king's cause
but for his own greater glory. He would be
an Alexander and crush the brethren
under his heel. You've seen the curled lip,
that contempt for whosoever would stand
against him. And now this braw gallant,
conqueror of the word, rides into Keith
on his Bucephalus – a spavined Sheltie.

How are the mighty fallen. He who was
arrayed in silks and falderals, like Solomon
in all his glory, appears before us
dressed in a torn red plaid. Brethren,
bear witness to this judgement, be sober
in your garments, wear only that which defends
against the elements, abjure ornament.
Let the righteousness of Christ be your
wedding garment – find it, oh find it
brethren in the rapturous sweetness of prayer.

And now, by God's grace, this man
of fantastic vanity, this malignant, has fallen
into our hands. He has hunted your sons
and fathers like dogs, merciless in their pursuit
even through the vineyard of the Lord. Beloved,
Remember what Amalek did unto thee

as ye came forth out of Egypt; how he met
thee by the way and smote the hindmost
of thee, all that were feeble and behind thee,
when thou wast faint and weary; and he feared
not God his punishment. Were you there
when he fell like the pestilence, laid waste
our fields and towns, fired our habitations.
Heard ye not your shrieking wives and daughters?

Silken tongued as the Serpent, preposterous
in his ambition, zealous in treachery,
a Judas who betrayed the Covenant
and bought with his thirty pieces of silver
preferment in the court of an idolatrous
and perfidious prince. Brethren, even
as Samuel smote Agag, rent him in pieces
and left him to the dogs, to the fowls of the air,
so let us hasten this traitor to judgement … '

'Rail on, Rabshekah,' Montrose protests
and turns his back. The brethren stunned –
the Minister's judgement thrown back
in his face. That black authority extinguished –
the fire and brimstone. For once Mr Kinanmond
is lost for words. Folk turn and stare
at the Graham. The escort hurries him away.

JOHN WILSON, DOMINIE

Aberdeenshire, May 1650

'Here comes James Graham, a traitor to his
  country.'
                    The Covenant Herald

How a man or woman will still
a room, draw eyes to form
or feature – or something unaccountable.
General Leslie would make his Progress
a humiliation. If he'd been hang-dog,
bowed in submission, the mobs
would have bayed. There were shouts
here and there but his dignity
survived the drawn face, the exhaustion.
The tragic is strangely exalted.

And they remember the beheading
of their King. The horror struck
deep in their blood. Gorges
rise at the Kirk's fanatics, the betrayal
of Scotland's freedom. To survive,
you turn as the wind blows.
But you have your thoughts. In the forum
of your heart, curse all authority.

And folk there are with nothing
to lose, who live like rats
starving under hovels of turf

and sticks, who sleep by their few
scrawny beasts for warmth.
Fodder, they are for Kirk or rebel
and nothing of their choosing. What,
for them, is the godly society? A few
crones for a burning? What,
for them, is the meaning of freedom?

Do they think the death of Montrose
will end it? Beyond all creeds
and kings is the question:
how to feed your bairns in a world
bereft of sense and reason.
Pillage or the Estates' taxes –
where do you turn? You're walking
a storm-swept, winter beach
that sucks your feet from under you.

THE TRIUMPH OF CAESAR

May, 1650

Once life had glittered, his youth
afire with tales of Caesar and his legions.
He'd dreamed of laurel crowns,
the Triumphus through cheering Rome.

Down through Aberdeenshire,
in the midst of a troop of dragoons,
the Graham rides an old carthorse.

The Colonel commanding the escort
is a severe but decent man –
with a taste for irony. He'd fought
with Leslie at Philiphaugh. Neither
had stomach for wanton slaughter.

They'd tried to save camp followers –
but the ministers had prevailed. Mile
on mile the Covenanters butchered –
remembering Kilsyth but a month
before – ripped women open,
left bairnies about to be born
kicking in their mothers' blood.
They filled mass graves
with Irish prisoners – who'd been given
quarter – drowned women

and children at Linlithgow. 'In the name
of Christ, let us cleanse this country
of malignants and their hideous spawn.
They carry the mark of the Beast.'

Each has a wary respect. Over
the miles they converse – soldiers
together. He's read of the Graham's
campaigns, owns Wishart's
Latin text – a copy from Amsterdam.
Even now, he can catch the air
of effortless command, the iron will,
suffers the scrutiny of the piercing eyes –
and in spite of all, there's the charm.
But he knows fine well his weaknesses –
careless intelligence, arrogance
amidst peers, wishful thinking.

'Know thine enemy' – *The Art of War*.

THE KING'S LIEUTENANT

Philiphaugh, September 1645

After Kilsyth, Glasgow had welcomed
Montrose. Looting was proscribed –
he hanged transgressors. Rich
pickings. Beyond their imaginings.
They saw pillage as their right.
But how to win hearts and minds
with an army of Highland reivers?

That intersection of two worlds:
Highland – Lowland; the warriors'
code and settled virtues,
the great sectarian divide –
and mutual abomination.
Did he dream Kilsyth was victory?

The executions fester. At Bothwell
the Highlanders melt away –
there's unfinished business in Argyll.
MacColla promises to return,
moves out with his spoils –
his knighthood. They never meet again.

So the frail weave unravels:
two thousand Irishes lost;
touchy Aboyne returned north
with his Gordons; the King's force
ambushed on its way to Scotland –

destroyed by Cromwell; the Border
earls too canny – for who would risk
all on this faltering venture?
And General Leslie on the march.

The haughs of Ettrick Water
are thick with Autumn fog.
Massacre looms out of the morning.

' … thou shalt save alive nothing
that breatheth: but thou
shalt utterly destroy them … '

EXILE

Stonehaven, 3rd September, 1646

*'I assure you that I no less esteem your willingness
to lay down arms at my command for a gallant
and real expression of your zeal and affection for my
service than any of your former actions …
For there is no man … that is ignorant that the rea-
son which makes me at this time send you out of the
country, is that you may return home with greater
glory … Wherefore I renew my former directions of
laying down arms unto you …'*

Charles R. 15th June, 1646

The North Sea brought to a roar, waves
rasping up the sand, a darting moon.
Up to their waists, two sailors
set a ship's boat pitching
through the glittering surf. They labour
in grudging seas out into the roads
of Stonehaven. The few, dim lights
in the town tug at the Graham's heart.

He'd visited Magdalen's grave at Kinnaird.
Remembered. The parks of Strathmore
were gold with bending oats. At Auld Montrose,
said farewells to his younger children.
Jean's eyes engaged – took his measure.
Smiled. An encounter of equals – as both
of them knew. Robert, shy and wary.
What soldier's, courtier's language would reach?

In Montrose the harbour had been strangely
empty. He'd read the Covenanters'
game – bent on delaying his departure
beyond his period of grace. Poured
from a tavern, a drunken captain had
offered a passage – could refit his ship
in three days. Those shifty, bloodshot eyes.
The exiles decided to make for Stonehaven.

They passed through Kineff and the lands
of Dunnottar – country they'd despoiled.
Blackened gables – an eerie darkness.
Seas were breaking in thunder
on the castle rock. Now in the roads they lift
and plunge. Lift and plunge. He grabs
a ship's ladder. They're bound for Bergen,
across the moonlit tumult to Norway.

In the thump and judder he tastes
the spice of danger but the hours that follow
bring an unexpected freedom – for he's put
his life entirely in another's hands.
He'd seen in the skipper a man he could trust.
The burden of months is falling from him.
Beneath his feet, the deck is alive –
his spirit stirs in the scudding wind.
When the king had directed to lay down
his arms he'd fought his disbelief.
Scotland ravaged – blood and suffering,
rending despair. And he'd lost all –
estates, fortune, Johnny. For nothing?

He saw his king as vacillating, weak,
lost to a dream of himself – not
first among equals – that honoured vision.

To sail from his beloved country –
it had seemed that nothing worse could follow.
But with sea miles gathering behind him,
hope flickers from the ashes – to free
the Faith from fanatics, to be reconciled
with the Kirk, to have a strong monarch
accountable to parliament. He challenges himself
to find joy, to restore his love of life.

THE GRAHAM IN THE MEARNS

15th May, 1650

We pass Stonehaven into the Mearns.
The Hawthorn in new leaf,
larks and peesies up. Wide
skies. By the burnsides, butterflies
chase amongst celandines.

Two wee lassies are playing
by the wayside. They throw handfuls
of sun-dried leaves into the breeze,
run shrieking after. They stop.
Stand. Stare at the passing sodjers.

Those eyes. Not only the child
grows – but the beholder.

Too late I understand the loss.

Green, so green. The parks
are flowing under a warm wind.
Between the muirs, the North Sea
dazzles behind the kirk at Inverbervie.

My last Spring. Never
so intense. Beyond failure
the great simplicities cry out –
and the merle's song like a wound.
Something settles in my soul.

The time of black flags –
Carbisdale – the incubus –
has passed.

    May I remember
this moment at the last.

MAGDALEN, MARCHIONESS OF MONTROSE

Kinnaird, Autumn 1645

And then we were married. So little
we really knew of one another.
My mother arranged it – our neighbour,
from a mile away, the young Montrose.
We'd played as children. He lived
for shooting, fishing – his horses.
A handsome boy – so full of himself.
Not tall. But perfect in proportion.

Wherever he went he was conscious,
somehow, of completing the picture.
I was flattered. Beguiled. In the first
months of marriage, after the starched
rituals of courtship, we'd wander
the parks of Kinnaird, share our dreams
by the glassy river, watch the dipping
swallows – exult in their freedom of the skies.
He'd read me his poetry. But now I wonder
where I was in his words. For I see
in the well-turned verse just another
display of the peacock. The bairns –
he'd hardly notice. When he did he'd
bewitch them. I'd feel a pang of jealousy.
Merely their mother. The healthy mare.

Father says he betrayed the Covenant.
I've never fully understood the matter
but imagine Jamie's own bewitchment –
that long, sad face of the king –
and Launcelot won by his Arthur. Or he'd see it
as his Rubicon – a Caesar he would be.
And he has his vision – church and state
and monarchy in balanced order –
but what price balance for a man
who'll never compromise? 'No middle way,'
he'd say to me, 'No middle way.'

And so there were tensions. Did ever
they come to words? I've heard tell,
in Glasgow, they had a fair strushie
at a General Assembly – 'a rash
and vainglorious young man'. My father's
wise, deeply considers – though no zealot,
he's made his peace with the Covenant –
and the Graham like the flash of a meteor.

He's left me landless, a pauper
in my father's house, took Johnny
to his death – so young, too
young for blood. His father's son
and never mine. And my bonny
Jamie, still a child, held
in plague-ridden Edinburgh Castle.

Wide skies – woods on woods, the landscape
featureless. This elegant confinement.
A few years of a life – then he'd gone.

I cultivate my flowers, my physic garden.
The Countess of Strathmore has passed me
a recipe for syrup of Bugloss.

It prevails, they say, against melancholy.

REMEMBERING KINNAIRD, 1630

Love came laughing through their springtime
though always the eyes of Persephone
carried a memory of winter. Spring
would hesitate behind drifts of rain

then smile in primroses by the forest's edge,
in nodding bluebells and kingcups
bright in the haughs where kine
grazed resurgent grasses.

But her eyes would settle on a distance far
beyond the flowers. What country did she reach?
Could she read the soaring swallows' dreams –
or touch their winter premonitions?

Even in summer's glory she'd seek out
the cailleach and cross her palm with silver.
But if she saw the future, what strength of love
was it, held her to the bitter course?

ROBERT GRAHAM

Kinnaird, 15th May, 1650

My aunties say I'm grandpa's image
and Jean, her father's spark –
she worships him. She doesn't suffer
fools, tholes no argument.
Beware when her eyes flash.

Now and then father thinks to step
into our lives – that habit of command.
My mother was abandoned – I've heard
the ladies talking. They say she burned
all father's letters. And Johnny dead.
They say it killed my mother. And Jamie
imprisoned in Edinburgh Castle.

Sometimes grandpa takes me hawking
and the gillie and I go fishing. Out
of the seething blackness of the Esk
we watch the silver salmon leap –
their glittering moments in the sun.

THE CHAPLAIN TO SOUTHESK

Kinnaird, 15th May, 1650

Montrose had an hour – a concession
from the Colonel. Talks to the Earl
in his library, says goodbye
to the children. This stranger, pale
and haggard – where was their father?
He talks of honour and duty.
Uncomfortable, formal moments
that leave them distressed and bewildered.
They're beyond the soldier's reach.

And their mother, lost in the winter
of her desolation, so long, so far away.
What guilt they carry – the innocents.
Beyond consolation. Perhaps the depths
can separate us from the love of God.
Southesk would bristle, 'Lassie, lassie,
tak a tummle tae yersel. Whar's
yer smeddum?' But what life
had she known, grown sickly in the shade
of men who cast such strong shadows?

The old Earl has played a canny game,
stayed aloof as it was safe to be,
saved what he could from his son-in-law's
wreckage. Ice and fire they are.
But he's not without wry humour –
and a father to his grandchildren.

He'd despaired of the Graham's arrogance –
a lucky soldier he says.
He's stern, judicious, shrewdly plays
his antagonists' weaknesses, knows
fine well that behind the Estates
it's not God but Mammon who rules.

AT THE HOUSE OF GRANGE, MONIFIETH

15th May, 1650

'I glory in what I have done though heartily
grieved that I have failed in setting the
Marquis free. On my head therefore expend
all vials of your wrath.'

Lady Grange

Eyes lowered, head bowed,
a grey ghost passes through the Hall –
the Graham in a cloak and gown
of the mistress. By the doors,
three sentinels are slumped
over muskets, drunk to snoring.

He holds his breath.

                Then out
into freedom and the gloaming, a warm,
wholesome night scented
with Scots Roses. And there,
vivid to his mind, the gardens
of Kinnaird. She might well
have been a widow, that lost girl.
Loved – but not cherished.

A moon path wrinkles
across the firth. Once
they'd walked to the stars.
A dog barks along the shore.
Shrill cries break
above the village – here,
now
     there –
from a bewildered twilight.

A flock of oystercatchers
in anguished
               dispossession?
Or souls
        in their first
bewilderment
           cut loose?

Then out of the shadows
beyond the gateway –
'Cam here yi
whoor. Let's hae
a grip o' ye.' And a staggering
trooper, half-seas over,
grabs him round the waist –
that metallic breath in his face.

'By Christ it's the Marquis.'
He holds a pistol to his belly. 'Hi!
Wee Jimmy! Eck! We hae
a richt sonsie quean here!

Efter you, your ladyship.'

Back through drunken laughter.

A PACK OF NAKED RUNAGATES

Dundee, 6th April, 1645

Showers on the wind. The wide firth
fretting. Short waves against
a flood tide. Contrary forces.
In a stiff westerly the King's standard
unfurled on the Law. The town at their feet.

He'd arrived at the West Port in a lather –
a chield ridden from Auchterhouse –
'The meenister telt me to tell ye that the hosts
of the Midians have cam oot o' the nicht
an' they're weel past Tullybaccart.'

Bells ring out from St Mary's steeple,
the militia are raised and able townsfolk.
They've heard tell of a massacre in Aberdeen.
The ports are closed. They man the ramparts.
But the wall by Corbie Hill is in disrepair.

The Irishes take a bastion. Turn the guns
and rake the town. The lean-jawed wolves
of Clan Donald break like the sea
along the Nethergate, flood the Market –
the hospital in flames and Bonnet Hill.

Montrose, had made his calculation – sack

a town to placate his caterans. And Dundee –
rich pickings. For the cause of a King.

Did he pause? No battlefield – but sword
and torch carried into the heart of lives,
their few bit comforts, their intimacies.

Did his God weigh in the scale of his judgement?
'Inasmuch as ye have done it unto one
of the least of these my brethren … '

They slaughter their way down the Murraygate,
hunt through lanes and closes, batter
through doors. Crazed on blood and claret,
spit men and women and children.

She heard the bells
and cannon thunder –
that shock for the heart.

Last night
a blood-red moon
had hung over the firth.

And this morning,
her neighbour,
Margaret Ritchie,
reported, that as midnight
had struck, the witch,

Grissell Jaffray,
had been seen talking
with the dead in the Howff.

Running feet –
and a pig squeals
down the wynd.
An urgent knocking.

'Mrs Scrimgeour,
Mrs Scrimgeour,
the runagates have fired
St Mary's.'
        Stealthy
at first – a thin
veil of smoke.
Then the acrid stench
of burnings.
        Gunshots.
A shrieking terror
silenced.
     And granny
into the box bed
with the weans.
        Then they're up
the turnpike stair
and the door broken in.
And the children – that full-

throated, chest-
heaving, red-faced,
desperate cry.

She can only crush
them to her bosom.

The panel of the bed
slides open.

There are three. The one
with wild eyes
fires his musket
at a cherub painted
on the ceiling, slashes
with his bloodied dirk
at a tapestried chair.

At that pitch of terror
a fair-haired, bull-strength
MacDonald grasps
the offending arm,
kneels by the bed – they
could be his own –
and strange as blessings
falling through a dream,
quietly sings
in a language that soothes
like a summer sea:

Gun gléidheadh gàirdean gaolach thu,

gum pògadh solas maidne thu

May loving arms hold thee,
the light of morning kiss thee,
meadow flowers dandle thee,
the climbing lark sing for thee.

May the grace of the swan be yours,
laughter of the dappled burn.

May Mary's blessings keep thee,
God's love light your way.

Then they're into the kists and
off down the stair
with burthens on their backs –
linens, lace,
buckled shoes,
a pair of ornate pistols,
clinking claret,
two pecks of meal
and moon-broad
silver plates.

Through smoke and turmoil,
looming through apocalypse,
Montrose would call off the pack
at their kill. For the Covenant army,
marched from Perth, approach

the West Port. Bullying,
cajoling, the sergeants labour
to gather their clansmen
while mounted above them,
the grey-eyed Graham sits
studied in his air of cool authority.

It's troopers' musket shots
that finally persuade. Bent
under plunder the caterans
stagger through the Cowgate Port.

A cold wind drifts
darkness along the North Sea.
Gold, from the West, the last
light streams under torn cloud,
the heights hinting that somewhere
there might even be serenity.

A man who knows beauty.

The fire of his rear-guard
recalls to duty. Montrose
falls back, directs
his defence. Order resolves
out of chaos. Hurry's dragoons
are beaten back. Montrose
takes the track to Arbroath.

–

As night falls, the last of the Covenant

army clatter through. Then up
and down the echoing wynds
Kirsty Scrimgeour hunts for her daughter.
That morning, at the back of nine,
Lizzie had gone up to the Hilltown
to find a new hat. Distraught,
through the flickering dark,
her mother searches the blind alleys
of her nightmare. 'Rob, have you seen
our Lizzie?' Breath heaving, hair
plastered in sweat, in despair
she stumbles home to the Overgate.
Down in the kitchen, the scullery maid
gives her a look. There, crouching,
rocking in the ingle neuk,
is her Lizzie, half naked,
an eye blackened, livid
cheeks, bruises along her thighs.
A log falls in the grate.
Shadows lance across the walls.

When they close their wakeful eyes
in the night's exhausted silence,
sights spring up – the High Street
a shambles – the gutted and the limbless
strewn. And within the fevered
wasteland of their dreams, sounds
and smells relentlessly harry –
in the Hospital of the Holy Trinity

the old and sick were burned
alive.
      They wake from sweating
turmoil, shouting in the dark.

But in spite of all, the world
abides.
      In the early light
an edge of cloud
is luminous as forked lightening –
their jealous God has spoken.

A man who's walked for days
has brought black cattle
down through Clova to the Market.
He stands bewildered. The milling
beasts are restless. His dog
snuffs the air and whines.
Timber yards on the wharves
still smoulder. A Norwegian ship
looks on, then tacks away.
Gulls clamour and
                wheel.

All day a slow procession –
the lucky in shrouds, knotted
at head and feet. At Roodyards,
the grave pits quickly fill.
Eight hundred dead, they say.

ESCAPE

6th and 7th April, 1645

Move and counter move. General Baillie's
heart quickens. Montrose will head
for Glen Esk – his passage to the Highlands.
'I'll have him – trapped between me and the sea.'
He deploys his troops across the roads to Brechin.

Bone weary, through the bristling dark,
the caterans pick a wary passage behind
Bailie's patrols. Montrose had led them
seventy miles. They'd sacked a town.
Abandoned trophies litter their way.

They collapse on the lawns of Careston Castle.

Pistol cracks.
         Shocked

             awake
by Covenant dragoons the dead
                  rise,
fight desperate, rear-guard skirmishes
to make the few miles to the glen –
where Covenant cavalry won't follow.

They'd lifted a few cattle by Auchmull.
An old woman had fallen on her knees
and cursed them. Safe by evening,
they trudge past black Loch Lee.

The bleat of snipe from the bogs is uncanny –
bird of the fairies, dangerous spirits.

Green hills, there are, of the mind
where a warrior might vanish, held
in thrall to waking nightmares.

A snatch of low sun. But the braes
still brown and ochre – Spring
not fully awake. The hag has worried
the camp followers' children – they see her
in shadows behind rocks, hear her
in a falcon's raucous yakking. They shiver
in a wind from Grampian snowfields.

They camp near the Falls of Unich
on grassy slopes under the sheltering crags
of Hunt Hill. The women had collected
birch wood from along Glen Esk.
A beast slaughtered. Bellies filled.
Stars are singing through the Highland dark.
For the few awake, a bard begins their stories.

Finn, the white haired, has the wisdom
of salmon. They need their giant-killing
heroes – their battle cunning, magic spears –
the distraction of other worlds. Life
on the edge – it offers no quarter.

DUNDEE

16th May, 1650

Five years since – and the town
still crippled. The unrelieved poor
survive in ruinous hovels.
God's plaguey visitations
have fallen on a sinful people.
How much can poor souls carry?

For months the markets were closed,
the merchants' booths empty.
Better the devil Montrose
than the fatal unseen? For instead
of insult and indignation he passes
through silence. And the burgesses
have given him a suit of good
broadcloth, befitting his rank.

THE MARQUIS ON PASSAGE

Dundee to Leith, 17th–18th May, 1650

Out into the firth. A stiff nor'east breeze
and a floodtide – slow progress.
We sail into the past – east
by Broughty Castle. We band of students
would take the ferry from Tayport,
set up butts on Broughty links.
Even now, as we pass that shore,
the wind carries our shouts and laughter.

Waves are breaking along the Abertay Bank –
ribs of weeded hulks comb
the purling tide. Spray spits.
I look into the seething jaws –
and wonder. We heel. With shouts
and heaves and groaning timbers,
go about, beat to windward.

To the west, Buddon Ness and the dear,
green braes of Angus and beyond,
like something at the edge of thought,
the Grampians' blue ridges.
My boyhood was the land – its wooded
glens, its dark and tumbling rivers,
its cold and windy heights – and the land,
my spirit – whatever in me is strong.

Once crossed the bar, we bear south
for St Andrew's Bay. Hills drop
behind – this slow and deepest severance.

From this exile there is no return.

The wind in a better quarter.
Too swift the passage. Gannets
plunge – lethal, direct, pure
purpose. Alasdair MacColla
how I lament for you.

Memory resolves to stone – the stark,
twin turrets of the red cathedral ruin,
St Rule's tower, and my alma mater –
that Island of Lotus Eaters. Oh I read
the Roman poets, histories and romances
but neglected serious study. Too busy
with club and bow, my horses –
Cupar races – feasts and entertainments,
the attention of young ladies.
I kept a box for their scented letters.

Too much came to me too soon.
Though it seems, now, to have been
an innocent time – before the foundations
shook, set soul against soul.
Argyle had been at St Salvator's – that strange,
shilpit creature – and David Lesley –
an able, decent soldier, once a friend.

Then the dogs in us were set loose.
Fife Ness – and soon I'll see the Isle
of May. And on the morrow – Leith.

EDINBURGH

18th May, 1650

They brought him by the Watergate.
In a cold drift from the North Sea
haar flowed round the Canongate steeples.
They'd thought for the women of Edinburgh
to stone him, tied his arms
to a chair in the hangman's cart to leave
his head exposed. Out of the fog
he trundled, the man who'd slaughtered
husbands and sons. Did the chill
temper their fire? Even the ministers'
exhortations failed against the rock
of that dignity. Weans stood silent,
thieves' hands were stilled. Dream
slow their progress. As they passed
Argyll's lodging Montrose looked up
but the eyes at the balcony shifted away.
That sleekit face – the mind's reflection.
Unscrupulous, crafty and skilful in politics,
wedded to his creed – but solicitous
in his care of wife and family.

Two men were never more asunder.

Loosed from the cart at the Tolbooth
the Graham gave the hangman gold
for a dram. The sun broke through.
This life – the theatre of the soul.

ARCHIE CAMPBELL, THE MARQUIS OF ARGYLL, AT HIS WINDOW

18th May, 1650

Charles is young, naïve – would trade
his own mother for his ends,
listens to his coterie of fools.
He's hedged his bets: by settlement
win Scotland by peaceful means
or by arms, through Montrose.

What drives the Graham? He's lost all.
He's wedded to principle and men
such as these are always self-deceived,
their thirst for power decked out
in moral trappings. He's laid waste
Argyll, slaughtered our clansmen,
roofs have been burned over women
and children. My motives, at least,
are straightforward: to seek
to establish Christ's Kingdom
on earth. The enemies of Christ
are my enemies, my methods simple
statecraft – I've studied 'The Prince'.
And if power falls to me –
so be it. I'm but God's instrument.

Were it not for the passions
of the Marquis, his military zeal,
his danger to the stability of Scotland,

it might not have been expedient
to send the King to the English
Parliamentarians – and execution.
For that's the truth of it. None
but a fool could have dreamed otherwise.
So one man's arrogance –
that instrument of Satan – destroyed
the possibility of accommodation.

My sources in The Hague inform he might
have married a princess. The man's
a fool. Caesar has come to grief.

God's mill grinds slow but sure.
And Cromwell played into my hands –
invaded Ireland – the Catholics
'engaged'. No hope for Charlie
there – so he agreed: Catholicism
not to be tolerated anywhere
in the kingdom. He'll annul all
recent treaties and commissions.

So the Graham was cut loose.
Thirty thousand pounds I put
on his head – he was duly delivered.

PENELOPE SENDS TO ODYSSEUS

Princess Louise
The Hague, Spring 1649

Resolved to your course
you set sail every moment,
your mind away.

Yet will you leave
a corner of your heart
for pale Penelope?

My own course is set.
Just once, once
and forever.

My vista is an empty
sea – grey-blue
your eyes, my voyager.

You sail into the whirlwind.
Jaws will gape.
And never a homecoming.

Louise

AT PARLIAMENT HALL

8am. Monday, 20th May, 1650

'… the most cruel and inhuman butcher
and murderer of his nation …'

"James Graham, you will be called to the bar
of Parliament to answer for your manifold
sins and to face judgement. We are here
this morning to advise so that you may appear
in a better light. First, your demeanour,
your arrogance must surely stand in your way.
Secondly, your personal vices are well
attested – principally, concupiscence,
your notoriety in the matter of women.
You are an affront to a godly society.
Thirdly, you have raised a civil war
in our country at the cost of thousands
of our brethrens' lives. Fourthly, in pursuit
of this deadly end you have sought the aid
of Popish, Irish cutthroats. Fifthly,
your caterans have been set to sack
and pillage. Women have suffered outrage,
children have been slaughtered. What say you?

You will be freed from excommunication
if you admit to the errors of your ways."

"Sirs, like all men in our fallen state,
my sins are many. But who can defend
against malice, the serpent tongue? You can
adduce no evidence that would stain
my character. As for war, I fought
with all diligence for the Covenant.
Do you recall what we signed? 'We declare
before God and men, that we have no
intention nor desire to attempt anything
that may turn to the dishonour of God, or
to the diminution of the king's greatness
and authority.' I have never strayed
from my faith and would find my soul's
peace in reconciliation with the Kirk.
But in the face of self-aggrandisement
and the manifest corruption of those
who would be leaders of our suffering
country, who shelter under the name of God,
I sought to defend justice, ancient right
and our martyred king. What fault was there?
No battle is fought without blood,
and no matter the diligence of commanders,
at times disorder will prevail. Only
hypocrites would deny the nature of war.
My cause was just, its execution, tempered
by my human failings. And when you entered
into a League and Covenant against
our king, my duty to oppose you was clear.
Everything I have done was in his name."

"James Graham, do you not yet understand
that against a king's law, or the perversion
of a plurality of votes, God's law must,
and will, prevail? Christ Jesus is King
and kings are His subjects. Showing no sign
of repentance, your excommunication stands.
We pass you to the judgement of the Estates
And thence to the judgement of Almighty God."

Called to the bar, he kneels
for sentence: to be hanged
at the Mercat Cross,
the body to hang three hours,
head, hands and legs
to be cut off, the trunk
to be buried at the Boroughmuir
by the hangman.

ARCHIBALD, LORD NAPIER, THE GRAHAM'S NEPHEW, REMEMBERS.

'So great attempts, heroic ventures shall
Advance my fortune or renown my fall.'
Montrose

It would have been an easy complicity
to surrender to his reputation, become
a Marshal of France or fulfil
his role as a Marshall of The Holy
Roman Empire, to have left Scotland
to its own infernal devices, to sojourn
in that court in exile, that nest of vipers
these smooth-tongued prancing rogues
assiduous only in pursuit of preferment,
in perfecting the sneer, but he cast
their dust from under his feet, repaired
to the Court of Elizabeth, Queen of Bohemia.

I marvel at what he achieved with a band
of wild caterans – but what glory
would have followed command
of the Emperor Ferdinand's army?
And after Magdalen's death, who knows
what might have unfolded.
For Princess Louise is a girl of mirth
and spirit, gifted, high-minded
untarnished by vanity. He made
her eyes shine. A child would have been

the king or queen of three kingdoms.
But the Graham would never relinquish
his duty to the martyred King.

He is a staunch friend, with a quick
intelligence, a slow-burning wit
an unfailing capacity to lift the spirit –
nothing daunts him. He inspires devotion.
In these last days his greatest yearning
is to be reconciled with the Kirk –
but a Church freed from the fever of theocracy.
He sought freedom of worship for all
and a monarchy accountable to law,
to constitutional government. He appeals
to reason. But what is reason to a ravaged
people, afire, at worst, with holy zeal,
in thrall to the prospect of Hell's pit?

I've heard him talk of the searing purity
of battle – beyond all creed or machination.
He felt more alive on the field of death
than anywhere else. And these grey eyes
would be fired by adversity – was Inverlochy
his sweetest victory? Beyond the sword,
where would such a man have found
fulfilment? Only the edge of steel
could match his temper. But fate conspired
against him – and he knew his betrayal.
Never one to weigh the odds,
honour would lead him open-eyed,
if not to victory, then to triumph in death.

EDINBURGH TOLBOOTH

20th–21st May, 1650

Through the night ministers
  berate him. 'Understand
ye not that in excommunication
  your soul hath been
delivered into the tormenting
  hands of the Devil?'
He suffers the fanatics to rave,
  unmoved by the prospect
of their Hell's fire. Though pale
  and weary, he can hardly
forbear from a smile. But dignity
  prevails. 'Gentlemen,
let me die in peace.' They leave,
  instruct his gaolers
to torment him – the stench
  of that pit would be
enough. In the early hours
  they're drunk to a stupor.
Through the sudden silence
  he hears the moans
of felons chained in their sores,
  drifts into a half-sleep.

Images flicker like moths
  through its twilight.
The house of Auld Montrose
  and a frost falling

through a rose-madder sunset
     loud with geese.
The air pure, keen as a blade.
     The distant hills
blue-black against the light.

     His mind shoulders
through his dreaming. Sins
     of omission weigh
heaviest. March at the windy
     Bog of Gight,
the Moray Firth grey-troubled
     and Johnny in his arms –
that laboured breath, the beaded
     sweat. His young
blue eyes liquid,
     fathomless. He holds
the boy as if to defy his passage.
     'I never knew
how much I loved that laddie.
     Too late
the dawning. How many pits
     have I filled? That fellowship
in death. But now I see all
     deaths are single –
and alone. These moments here
     I count as privilege.

And Magdalen – that good
     and haunted woman.
'Gin I speak wi the tungs

o men an angels,
but hae nae luve i my hairt,
   I am no nane
better nor dunnerin bress
   or a ringing cymbal'

Tumult in the street. Drums
and trumpets – my last day.

AT THE MERCAT CROSS

2.00 pm. 21st May, 1650

I'll not hang like a common
criminal – a scarlet cassock,
silver lace, a beaver hat.
Dressed like a bridegroom.

I leave them by the gallows.
Strange, in these moments –
a nagging regret that I'll pass
unshaven. This long climb …

No fear of death. Too often
I've looked in its face. But the weight
of thousands on my head?
Men died for my conviction.
I willed it. I hear the serpent
whispering – 'Jamie, Jamie –
for your own greater glory.'

God is just. I die to fulfil
the purposes He has ordained.

As for my flesh, its fate
will not be an event for me –
only for witnesses.
Crows and kites will be fed.

What have I feared? No man.
Only shame. Dishonour.

'Hangman, you've built a fine
scaffold – everyone to his trade.
'Here, I'll pay my dues to you … '

He stands on the platform, looks
round, an eagle at its eyrie –
that unflinching authority.
His arms are bound, a rope
knotted at his neck.
The hangman in tears.
'May God have mercy
on this afflicted kingdom.'

Then silence. Never so intense.
That sea of raised faces.

'Lord into thy hands I commend
my spirit.' And a flooding peace …

'Breathe deeply. The moment …

and the merle singing … '

BIBLIOGRAPHY

Bell, Robin: *Civil Warrior* (Luath Press Ltd, 2002).

Buchan, John: *The Marquis of Montrose* (Thomas Nelson and Son, 1913).

McKean, C., Harris, B., Whatley, C. (Eds): *Dundee, Renaissance to Enlightenment* (Dundee University Press, 2009).

Fraser, Murdo: *The Rivals* (Birlinn, 2015).

Tranter, Nigel: *The Young Montrose and Montrose: The Captain General* (Coronet Books,1997).

Williams, Ronald: *Montrose, Cavalier in Mourning* (Barrie and Jenkins Ltd, 1975).

Stevenson, David: *Highland Warrior: Alasdair MacColla and the Civil Wars* (John Donald, 2003).

Wedgewood, C.V.: *Montrose* (William Collins Ltd, 1952).